THE NEW CREATION IN CHRIST

Jerry Wilder, Sr.

Diligence Publishing Company
Bloomfield, New Jersey

To contact Jerry Wilder, Sr. to preach or speak at your church, organization, seminar, or conference email:

Jerry.Wilder213@yahoo.com

ISBN:979-8-9869173-9-9

Printed in the United States

TABLE OF CONTENTS

ACKNOWLEDGEMENTS

I would like to take this opportunity to acknowledge my loving wife Verdele and our family, who mean the world to me, and for allowing me the space and the time to write this book to be a blessing to the world.

I would also like to acknowledge my father Johnny and my mother Mamie, who are now in heaven, for teaching me the importance of a strong work ethic, and for teaching me right from wrong, because in today's world, people are calling right wrong and wrong right. They also taught me that whatever I start, to make sure I finish, and to never quit or give up, because quitters never win and winners never quit. I am eternally grateful for them.

INTRODUCTION

The purpose of writing this book is to inform believers everywhere about the new creation in Christ and the work of the Holy Spirit that takes place in the heart (spirit) of man upon one's confession of the Lordship of Jesus the Christ, according to Romans 10:9 - 10.

The Bible says in Romans 10:9-10, "That if thou shalt confess with thy mouth the Lord Jesus, and shalt believe in thine heart that God hath raised him from the dead, thou shalt be saved. For with the heart man believeth unto righteousness; and with the mouth confession is made unto salvation."

The challenge and struggle that many sincere Christians have, upon their confession of Jesus as Lord, is in their flesh. Because up to the point of receiving Jesus as Lord and Savior, your flesh has ruled, dominated, and dictated your life. As a matter of fact, feelings are the voice of the flesh, and the flesh will feel and say anything because your flesh is upset now that Jesus is Lord.

Hopefully, this book will help you see yourself in the light of God's Word. You have a new identity in Christ. You are a new creature in Christ if you have received Him as your Lord and Savior.

CHAPTER 1

YOU ARE A NEW CREATION

The Bible says in 2 Corinthians 5:17, "Therefore, if any man be in Christ, he is a new creature."

As stated in the introduction, according to Romans 10:9 the Bible says, "That if thou shalt confess with thy mouth the Lord Jesus, and shalt believe in thine heart that God hath raised him from the dead, thou shalt be saved."

Romans 10:10 says, "For with the heart man believeth unto righteousness, and with the mouth confession is made unto salvation."

The moment that anyone confesses the Lordship of Jesus and believes that God raised Him from the dead, they become a new creature in Christ. This is how God sees them. In order for the body of Christ to walk in victory it is imperative that the believer sees himself in the light of God's Word.

If you have confessed with your mouth the Lordship of Jesus, then that makes you a new creature! Say this to yourself, "I am a new creature."

If the believer is going to walk in the reality of the new creation, they must understand what the new creation is! The new creation is spiritual, and it takes place in the heart (spirit of the person) upon someone confessing with their mouth the Lord Jesus and believing in their heart that God raised Him from the dead. At that moment, the person's spirit is recreated by the Holy Spirit, and their spirit is made alive to God, therefore, making them a child of God.

One of the most amazing and remarkable things that takes place in the new creation experience is that one goes from a sinner to a child of God based on what they confess with their mouth and what they believe in their heart. Instantly, you are delivered from the power of darkness and translated into the Kingdom of His dear Son.

Upon your confession of the Lordship of Jesus, your life is so totally transformed that initially people who know you won't believe what has transpired in your life because they knew you when.

People often underestimate the power of God. Philippians 1:6 states, "Being confident of this very thing, that He who has begun a good work in you will complete it until the day of Jesus Christ."

If you are born again, the new creation in Christ is the beginning of the good work He has begun in you.

God works from the inside out. Your spirit is made instantly alive to God. and God begins and completes the process of His transformative work in your life.

Spiritually speaking, you are placed by the Holy Spirit back into the position Adam had with God before he fell from God's grace.

Thank God for the new creation in Christ.

As believers, most of the body of Christ understands that upon the confession of the Lordship of Jesus, we are new creatures and our sins are forgiven. What we, the body of Christ, do not realize is that at the same time God forgave us of our sins; He imparted into our born- again recreated human spirit, His nature. 2 Peter 1:4 says every believer is a partaker of God's divine nature.

Every child of God has God's nature, His life and ability, on the Inside. My God! You are not who you used to be! Without this impartation, the new creation would not be possible. In urban America, the changing of your name doesn't make you a new person, it's the changing of a man's heart that makes him anew.

The New Creation is so incredibly remarkable, that if anyone confesses with their mouth the Lord Jesus and believes in their heart that God raised Jesus from the dead, they are saved! At that moment, they become a new person spiritually on the inside.

During the process of salvation, your spirit – the real you – is born from above, born anew, and made alive with God because you are a new creature. The new creation is so awesome that as a child of God you can stand in the presence of God without guilt, without low self-esteem, without inferiority, and without condemnation and sin consciousness.

As a believer, you can stand in God's presence as if you have never sinned, because every sin in your life BC (before Christ) is forgiven and under the blood of Jesus as a new creature in Christ.

As a believer, your spirit has been recreated, and your sin nature has been eradicated by the Holy Spirit. Again, I say if you have confessed the Lordship of Jesus, you are a new creature in Christ. The new creation must become a living reality to you. The written Word of God must become the living Word on the inside of you. "Therefore, if any man be in Christ, He is a new creature: old things are passed away;

behold, all things are become new" (2 Corinthians 5:17).

The Bible says in John's Gospel chapter 1 verse 10, He was in the world, and the world was made through Him, and the world did not know Him. Verse 11 says, He came to His own and His own did not receive Him. Verse 12 Says, but as many as received Him, to them He gave the right to become children of God, to those who believe in His name. So in August the summer of 1983, I received Jesus Christ as my Lord and Savior, and I became a child of God.

Kingdom Principle: It's not enough to just believe. You must receive what you say you believe. There are a lot of people that believe, but "have they received?" is the question.

I did not grow up in church. I can count the times on one hand that I attended church. If my memory serves me correctly, and it does because I have the mind of Christ, those times

I attended church were Easter and Christmas. Because back when I was growing up, you always got new clothes (I always got a new suit and new shoes) for Easter and you wanted to wear your new Easter clothes and your new Easter shoes to church.

In spite of going to church on these special occasions as a child, I don't remember being taught very much about Jesus, but what I do remember is having a giant size Bible sitting on the coffee table in my living room that nobody ever read.

As I grew up and got older, from the age of 18 to 28 as a young adult, I realized something was missing from my life and that something that was missing was God Himself, even though I didn't know it at the time. I'm full of God today. I'm full of the Word and full of His Spirit, but back then there was an empty void in my life, and I tried to fill that void with smoking, drinking, drugging, and anything else I could think of only to discover after trying those things for so long, that the empty void was never filled. The only thing that smoking, drinking, and drugging did for me was left me feeling bad and with a hangover.

I did not realize until after Christ saved me, that God created man with a place in the heart of man for Himself and nothing and nobody could fill the empty void but God Himself. No cars, no women, no smoking, drinking, or drugging can fill that empty void as I have already said – nobody but God.

I grew up as a former high school basketball player. I love the game. I played it day and night. I love winning, and I excelled at the game. But what I realized was anything I attempted to do off of or away from the basketball court was complete failure. But things began to change when Jesus got my attention when I was 28 years old. I can recall it today as if it was yesterday. I had gone to church, and as I was in church, the Spirit of God said to me that if I would serve Him and be faithful to Him like I was to basketball, He would bless my life. At that moment, I committed to give my life fully to the Lord.

As an unsaved, unchurched, athlete, I understood commitment, faithfulness, and dedication, so for the last 42 years as a Christian, I have been faithfully serving Christ. God wastes nothing in our lives. Because of my training and conditioning during my many years as an athlete, I had practiced commitment, faithfulness, and dedication, so I was able to shift my commitment, dedication, and faithfulness from the game of basketball to my life as a Christan. God has been faithful to His word. Because of my obedience to serving Him with my whole heart, He has blessed my life just like He said He would. From my own experience, I can share with you that Christ is a game changer. I absolutely have no regrets whatsoever for giving my life to Christ. My life has purpose, meaning, and fulfillment.

The new creation in Christ is one of the most amazing, miraculous, and remarkable things to take place in my life. Jesus changed my life forever. I became a new creature in Christ. Making Jesus the Lord of my life was the best decision I ever made. Initially after my encounter with the resurrected Savior Jesus, I knew that something had happened to me even though I could not articulate what it was. I knew I was changed, and to my surprise I was able to begin to live the life I always wanted to live. Prior to my new creation experience, I did a lot of things to be a part of the in-crowd, to be accepted, and to fit in. When I shared the good news about my salvation with my family, they did not believe I was saved because they knew me. They knew what I used to do and how I was living, but over time, Jesus changed my walk and my talk. It was then that my family realized what had taken place in my life was more than just a phase.

The power of God had touched my life, changed me, and saved me.

When it comes to what God has done in my personal life, the new creation is now a living reality; I am who God said I am, and I can do what God says I can do.

CHAPTER 2

OLD THINGS ARE PASSED AWAY

Jesus was the first person to use the term, "You must be born again."

Jesus used this term in His conversation with Nicodemus. (John 3:3)

Jesus says to Nicodemus, "Except a man be born again, he cannot see the Kingdom of God." Jesus knew the spiritual condition of men, consider this statement Jesus made in John 3:6, "That which is born of the flesh is flesh, and that which is born of the Spirit is spirit."

Jesus was making reference to two types of birth: human physical birth, and the new birth of the human spirit. The Bible says in Romans 5:12, "Wherefore, as by one man sin entered into the world, and death by sin; and so, death passed upon all men, for that all have sinned."

Most Christians understand that the one man is Adam. Adam was the first man. Adam was a representative of the whole human race. The whole human race was identified with Adam, but when Jesus came, He identified with mankind. According to Philippians 2:7, the Bible says, "But he made himself of no reputation, and took upon him the form of a servant and was made in the likeness of men."

So, when Adam disobeyed God and died spiritually, we all died. Genesis 2:15-17 says, And the LORD God took the man and put him in the garden of Eden to dress it and to keep it. And the LORD God commanded the man, saying, Of every tree of the garden thou mayest freely eat: but of the tree of the knowledge of good and evil, thou shalt not eat of it: for in the day that thou eatest thereof thou shalt surely die."

Adam and Eve disobeyed God and ate of the tree of the knowledge of good and evil and thereby experienced spiritual death.

The whole human race was identified with Adam. The last Adam came in the person of Jesus Christ to fix up what the first Adam messed up. The Bible says in Romans 5:19, "For as by one man's (Adam) disobedience many were made sinners, so by the obedience of one (Jesus) shall many be made righteous."

The Gospel according to John says in John 1:1, "In the beginning was the Word, and the Word was with God, and the Word was God."

John 1:14 says, "and the Word was made flesh, and dwelt among us, (and we beheld his glory, the glory as of the only begotten of the Father.) full of grace and truth."

As previously stated, if any man confesses with his mouth the Lord Jesus and believes in his heart that God raised Him from the dead, he shall be saved. At that instant, he becomes a new creature, and old things are passed away. People love God, people are sincere, but many believers don't have an awareness of the old things that have passed away. Take some time to reflect on the list below of the old things that have passed away that applies to the life of the new creation:

1. Spiritual death – Passed away
2. Separation – Passed away
3. Alienation – Passed away
4. Condemnation – Passed away
5. Sin consciousness – Passed away

The new creation is one of the most incredible and amazing things to happen in the human heart. I reiterate, if any person confesses the Lordship of Jesus, there is an instant passing away and eradication of old things from their born again, recreated human spirit, making them a new creature in Christ.

I believe the term Jesus used when He spoke to Nicodemus, "You must be born again" and the term Paul used after his encounter with the resurrected Savior Jesus Christ, "You are a new creature in Christ," are synonymous.

As devastating and chaotic as creation was after the fall of Lucifer, as described in Genesis 1:2, "And the earth was without form, and void, and darkness was upon the face of the deep. And the Spirit of God moved upon the face of the waters," so were we in our spirits after the fall of Adam. Spiritual death reigned in our hearts because it passed upon all of mankind, for ALL have sinned. Because of the chaos, God had to speak to it to bring order. Genesis1:3 says, "And God said, "Let there be light: and there was light."

Genesis 1:4 says, "And God saw the light, that it was good."

Kingdom Principle: To regain order, any chaos must be spoken to.

The Bible says in Psalm 119:130, "The entrance of thy words giveth light."

The Bible says in 2 Corinthians 4:3-6, "But if our gospel be hid, it is hid to them that are lost: In whom the god of this world hath blinded the minds of them which believe not, lest the light of the glorious gospel of Christ, who is the image of God, should shine unto them. For we preach not ourselves, but Christ Jesus the Lord; and ourselves your servants for Jesus' sake. For God, who commanded the light to shine out of darkness, hath shined in our hearts, to give the light of the knowledge of the glory of God in the face of Jesus Christ."

We can praise God knowing that we are walking in the blessings and the newness of the new creation, and in the awareness of the old things that have passed away. Hallelujah.

CHAPTER 3

BEHOLD ALL THINGS ARE BECOME NEW

The word behold means to see a thing or person, especially something remarkable and amazing. That's what the writer of 2 Corinthinans 5:17 is trying to get the believer to see about the new creation in Christ! All things are become new. Every believer needs to see himself or herself anew.

To see oneself anew involves letting go of old beliefs and perceptions about who one is and that hold the person back from embracing him or herself as the new creation. The new creation has a new identity that has been redefined by Christ. When one sees him or herself anew, they turn away from the old self-defeating thought patterns and habits and embrace their new life in Christ.

The new creation in Christ is the greatest thing to ever happen to mankind: to have his human spirit to be recreated and made alive by the Holy Spirit upon his confession of the Lordship of Jesus Christ.

The apostle Paul wanted the saints to really behold and see what really took place internally from a spiritual perspective. The moment anyone confesses with their mouth the Lord Jesus and believes in their heart that God raised HIM from the dead, they shalt be saved.

At that moment they are born again, made alive, made spiritually anew, because in their human spirit, they have received eternal life. Behold, all things are become new. The man or woman that confesses the Lordship of Jesus becomes new. Wow, wow, wow. They have a new recreated human spirit. They are a partaker of God's divine nature.

God is a Spirit and everything God is, so are we as children of God. As children of God, we have the same physical body but a new recreated human spirit. "And you hath he quickened, who were spiritually dead in trespasses and in sins; wherein in time past you walked according to the prince of the power of the air, the spirit that now worketh in the children of disobedience: But God who is rich in mercy, for his great love wherewith he loved us, Even when we were dead in sins hath quickened us together with Christ (by grace you are saved)" Ephesians 2:1-5.

Behold all things are become new! You are not who you were. You were a sinner; now you are a child of God, recreated in the image and likeness of God. Every believer must see himself in the light of God's Word and live in the revelation of that truth.

You are a tripartite being: you are a spirit (the real you), you have a soul, and you live in a body. God recreated man in the spirit to have relationship and fellowship with Him. So, when God communicates with man, He speaks to his spirit, not his flesh because his flesh is not saved. God doesn't speak to man's head because his mind is not saved. His mind can only be renewed (read Romans 12:1-2).

The apostle Paul wrote, "I beseech you, Therefore, brethren, by the mercies of God, that you present your bodies a living sacrifice, holy, acceptable unto God, which is your reasonable service. And be not conformed to this world: but be ye transformed by the renewing of your mind, that ye may prove what is that good, and acceptable, and perfect, will of God (Romans 12:1-2).

Behold all things are become new.

CHAPTER 4

RECONCILED

The Bible says in 2 Corinthians 5:18 Now all things are of God who, has reconciled us to Himself through Jesus Christ.

There is nothing more important to God than to have man reconciled to Himself. God reconciled by faith the human race to Himself through Christ.

2,000 plus years ago, through His redemptive work, Christ, paid the price in full for the sin debt of humanity. The Bible says in Isaiah 53:6 "And the Lord has laid on Him the iniquity of us all."

My God! Everything that spiritual death made humanity become, was placed on our Lord Jesus Christ. The Bible says in the Gospel of John chapter 14 verse 6 that Jesus Himself says, "I am the way, the truth, and the life. No man comes to the Father except through Me."

The Bible also says, "Neither is there salvation in any other: for there is no other name under heaven given among men by which we must be saved" (Acts 4:12).

1 Timothy 2:4-5 says, "Who will have all men to be saved and to come unto the knowledge of the truth. For there is one God and one mediator between God and men, the man Christ Jesus."

Read 2 Corinthians 5:18 very carefully. It says, "who has (past tense) reconciled us." God didn't wait on man to get himself together to reconcile him. Man was spiritually dead and could not approach God. Now that we through Jesus Christ, have been reconciled to God Himself, the ball is in man's court, it is his call. The Bible says that if you confess with your mouth the Lord Jesus and believe in your heart that God has raised him from the dead; you will be saved.

It's only then at that moment that you being reconciled to God through Jesus Christ becomes a reality to you. It's at that moment that you become a new creature in Christ.

Have you ever thought about this? You twice belong to God! Initially, we all belonged to God before Adam sinned. After Adam disobeyed God, sin came upon us all and we were separated from God. (See Romans 5:12, 1 Timothy 2:13-14.)

Thank God Jesus came that we might be reconciled to the Father through Him. If you have confessed the Lordship of Jesus and believe God raised Him from the dead, then you are a child of God, and you are as much one with the Father as Jesus is Himself. You have been reconciled and as a believer, you have been given the ministry of reconciliation. Take a minute to think about that. As believers, God has given all of us the ministry of reconciliation. That is absolutely amazing! Every believer has already been given a ministry by God.

As a believer, you do not have to chase a title or pursue ministry to feel like you are somebody. Let me tell you, you are already somebody. You are a new creature in Christ. Old things have passed away. You don't become any better than your new creation experience that is with or without a title. Believers everywhere must remember John 3:17, "For God did not send His Son into the world to condemn the world, but that the world through Him might be saved." Reconciliation is not just for those with titles or positions in the church. Reconciliation is the ministry of every born-again child of God.

CHAPTER 5

GOD WAS IN CHRIST

To wit, that God was in Christ reconciling the world unto himself! (2 Corinthians 5:19)

The Bible says in John 3:16 that God so loved the world that He gave His only begotten Son that whosoever believeth in Him should not perish but have everlasting life.

God so loved the world!!! Not the Church, that He gave the world a chance at everlasting life and a chance to have a relationship with Himself.

Hear what the Spirit of the Lord is saying in John 3:16. Jesus is talking about love, and He said, "For God so loved..." In this verse God did not give a reason for His love because the love of God is unconditional. God doesn't love you because of any particular reason. He loves you because He is love. As a matter of fact, love is not a feeling. Love is an action. So the verse lets us know who He loved which was the world and the action He took. The Bible says He gave. God gave all that He had. He gave the best of what He had, which was His only begotten Son, Jesus Christ, that you might be saved.

God is amazing. He is the eternal everlasting GOD. God is God. He doesn't need anyone's help to be God. He is all righteous by Himself, but the one thing He can never be by Himself is LOVE because LOVE must always have someone to LOVE. That's where you and I come into the picture. Read 1 John 4:8-11.

Thank you, Jesus, that the Word says that God was in Christ reconciling the world to Himself. Every member of the body of Christ at some point was in the world but now that we are saved, even though we are still in the world, we are not of the world.

The God and Father of our Lord Jesus Christ is the God of a second chance. How many times has He given all of us a second chance, a third chance, etc.?

I can remember in my life asking God and saying to Him, "O please, O please, O please gimme just one more chance," and of course He did because again, He is the God of a second chance.

God the Father is the author of eternal salvation. Salvation was His eternal plan from the beginning. He sent His Son Jesus to carry out and execute His eternal plan of salvation. He came and died for the world. The Bible says in Hebrews 10:12, "But this man, after he had offered one sacrifice for sins forever, sat down on the right hand of God."

After this perfect sacrifice of Jesus Christ, God Himself accepted it on behalf of all mankind and considered the claims of justice satisfied and every debt paid in full. Now God has a legal right to offer to mankind eternal life because man's debt has been paid in full. The world does not realize that God is not imputing their trespasses against them because "the God of this world hath blinded the minds of them which believe not, Lest the light of the glorious gospel of Christ, who is the image of God, should shine unto them" (2 Corinthians 4:4).

Through the redemptive work of God in Christ, every man and every woman has a right to be saved. Will everyone be saved? Probably not because some people will not freely give their lives to Christ to receive eternal life. "The Lord is not slack concerning his promise, as some men count slackness" (2 Peter 3:9).

You do not need to be called to five-fold ministry to be somebody, so don't feel compelled or pressured to go into this level of ministry unless there is a genuine authentic call of God on your life for five-fold ministry. Through Christ you are the new creation. You are already somebody. You are the best. Be true to your unique authentic self.

The Bible says, "The Lord is not slack concerning his promise, as some men count slackness, but is longsuffering to us-ward, not willing that any should perish, but that all should come to repentance" (2 Peter. 3:9).

Every child of God, every new creature, every person who has confessed the Lordship of Jesus has already been given a ministry. The church's responsibility is to let the world know that God was in Christ reconciling the world unto Himself. All the world has to do is come to Jesus. The Father has committed unto us (the body of Christ) the word of reconciliation. God was in Christ, and Christ through His Holy Spirit is in you. You have been given power to be a witness. Acts 1:8 says, "But you shall receive power when the Holy Spirit has come upon you, and you shall be witnesses to Me in Jerusalem, and in all Judea and Samaria, and to the end of the earth."

You have been given power to minister reconciliation to the world.

CHAPTER 6

AMBASSADORS FOR CHRIST

Now then, we are ambassadors for Christ, not for ourselves nor for our own kingdom but for His Kingdom. My hope is that every believer should know he or she is an ambassador for Christ. An ambassador for Christ is a Kingdom government official that understands that Jesus is the King of Kings and the Lord of Lords. It's about advancing His Kingdom in the earth realm.

The Kingdom of God is not a democracy, The Kingdom of God is a theocracy, and Jesus is both Lord and King.

As ambassadors of the Kingdom, you must seek first the Kingdom of God and His righteousness. God will provide for your needs. Jesus taught His disciples in Matthew

6:33 saying, "But seek ye first the kingdom of God and his righteousness and all these things shall be added to you."

In the verses leading up to Matthew 6:33. Jesus was teaching His disciples that believers are not to worry about food and drink or clothes. As a Kingdom representative and spokesperson, the King of kings will provide and add these things to your life. When you take care of God's business, God will take care of you.

Ambassadors are usually well taken care of and are first-class citizens. Every believer is an ambassador for Christ and has been given the ministry of reconciliation. As ambassadors, just as Jesus was about His Father's business, we the body of Christ must be about the family business – (souls). Proverbs 11:30 says, "The fruit of the righteous is a tree of life, and he who wins souls is wise."

Revelation 11:15 says "The kingdoms of this world have become the kingdoms of Our Lord and his Christ, and He shall reign forever and ever."

Never forget as a believer you are really a spokesperson for Christ. You are His mouthpiece and representative in the earth. You are on assignment as ambassadors for Christ, and you have a great work to do. As an ambassador, God wants to speak through you. God wants to use you to speak to those who are lost, hurting, or living their lives without Him. The scripture says in 2 Corinthians 5:20, "we are ambassadors for Christ, as though God were pleading through us to a dying and lost world. We implore you on Christ's behalf, be reconciled to God."

Even in this book, I am making an appeal to you. If you do not know Jesus Christ in a personal way and have never confessed with your mouth the Lordship of Christ, be reconciled with Him now.

You are one decision away from the greatest decision you have ever made in your life and the greatest move of God you have ever experienced. Again, I say be reconciled.

CHAPTER 7

CHRIST MADE SIN FOR US

Jesus was not born in sin, because His birth was miraculous. He was tempted from all points without sin. The scripture says the Father God "made him who knew no sin to be sin for us" (2 Corinthians 5:21).

He was made like us so that we could become like Him. Everything that spiritual death made humanity to be, Jesus became so that the Father could legally offer salvation to everyone. Anyone who would confess with their mouth the Lord Jesus and believe in their heart that God raised Him from the dead shall be saved. Just imagine, Jesus had never throughout eternity been separated from the Father, but when Jesus was made sin, He was separated from the Father. He died spiritually and became mortal (subject to death).

In the garden of Gethsemane, Jesus makes this powerful statement, "O My Father, if this cup cannot pass away from Me unless I drink it, Your will be done" (Matthew 26:42).

In John 6:38, Jesus Himself made this powerful statement, "For I have come down from heaven, not to do My own will but the will of Him who sent Me." Wow! Jesus came all the way from heaven, through 42 generations, wrapped in frail humanity to die for YOU and ME, that the Father would be pleased.

Jesus' heart desire was not to do His own will, but to do the will of the Father. To please the Father should be the desire of every believer! Jesus submitted His will to the will of the Father, willing to die for us, because justice demanded that the penalty for sin be paid in full, that the world might be given a chance to be saved.

As a believer, as a child of God, you should know that you are valuable. You are the apple of God's eye. Your life matters and it counts. You are and you were worth dying for. Jesus died that you might be reconciled to the Father through Him.

The devil tried to kill Jesus many times to make salvation impossible, but the devil could not kill Him, neither could any man take His life; Jesus had to lay His life down so that we, the people of God, the body of Christ, might have eternal life. Jesus says in John 15:13, "Greater love hath no man than this, that a man lay down his life for his friends."

What a blessing it is to be a friend of God. What a friend we have in Jesus.

Jesus made this statement in John 10:10 as He describes why He came, "The thief cometh not, but for to steal, and to kill, and to destroy: I am come that they might have life, and that they might have it more abundantly."

God has made salvation available to everyone. Salvation is free for us, but that does

THE NEW CREATION IN CHRIST

not mean it did not come with a cost. It cost God everything. Jesus was the first person to pass from spiritual death to spiritual life. He is the head of the new creation. 1 Peter 3:18 says "For Christ also hath once suffered for sins, the just for the unjust, that he might bring us to God, being put to death in the flesh, but quickened in the Spirit."

"For whosoever shall call upon the name of the Lord shall be saved. How then shall they call on him in whom they have not believed? And how shall they believe in him of whom they have not heard? And how shall they hear without a preacher? And how shall they preach; except they be sent? As it is written, how beautiful are the feet of them that preach the gospel of peace and bring glad tidings of good things" (Romans10:13-15).

CHAPTER 8

THE RIGHTEOUSNESS OF GOD IN CHRIST

The Bible says according to Romans 10:9, "That if thou shalt confess with thy mouth The Lord Jesus, and believe in thine heart that God hath raised him From the dead, thou shalt be saved." Romans 10:10 says, for "with the heart Man believeth unto righteousness, and with the mouth confession is made unto salvation."

At the moment you confess the Lordship of Jesus you are saved. You are a new creature in Christ. At that instant, you become the righteousness of God in Christ. Righteousness means to be in right standing with God. To be in right standing means you are in relationship with God. Many people today are saved but do not realize the reality of their righteousness in Christ. In order for us, the body of Christ, to come boldly to the throne of grace, that we may obtain mercy and find grace to help in time of need, every believer needs to have a revelation of the righteousness of God.

My heart's desire for the body of Christ is that every believer understands his or her righteousness in Christ. This is what the apostle Paul had to say about the righteousness of God according to Romans 3:21-24, "But now the righteousness of God apart from the law is revealed, being witnessed by the Law and the Prophets, even the righteousness of God, through faith in Jesus Christ, to all and on all who believe. For there is no difference; for all have sinned and fall short of the glory of God, being justified freely by His grace through the redemption that is in Christ Jesus."

Tradition has placed an emphasis on "all have sinned and come short of the glory of God." However, the Spirit of God through the apostle Paul emphasized righteousness through faith in Jesus Christ. As a believer, you have been justified (declared righteous). You! Yes, I'm talking to you. You are the righteousness of God in Christ. Forgive yourself because God already has. Stop putting yourself down or beating yourself up because you are in right standing with God.

Every child of God should understand that they can stand in the presences of God as if they have never ever committed a sin, because their sins are under the blood of Jesus. That is a strong powerful statement, such a statement will shake up your religion if you are religious.

Christianity is not a religion – it's a personal relationship with God the Father through Jesus Christ. The fact that, as Christians, we are able to stand in the presence of God without guilt or condemnation is quite remarkable. The Bible says, "There is therefore, now no condemnation to those who are in Christ Jesus, who do not walk according to the flesh, but according to the Spirit" (Romans 8:1).

Remember you are not just an old sinner saved by grace. You are a child of God. Righteousness is instantaneous, but holiness is progressive. Righteousness doesn't make you perfect.

You do not obtain righteousness by keeping the mosaic law. The law has been fulfilled and laid to the side by the atoning sacrifice of Jesus Christ. We, the body of Christ, the Church of God, have been given a new law. Jesus said, "A new commandment I give unto you, That you love one another; As I have loved you, that you also love one another. By this shall all men know that you are my disciples, if you have love one to another" (John 13:34-35).

You do not obtain righteousness by human effort or good works. Now we should do good works because the Bible says in Ephesians 2:10, "For we are his workmanship, created in Christ Jesus unto good works which God hath before ordained that we should walk in them."

You are made the righteousness of God in Him for with the heart man believeth unto righteousness. As a believer, you are the righteousness of God in Christ. God is not mad at you. He is not angry with you. He has nothing to pay you back for. If you are a believer, everything you have ever done is under the blood. "I, even I, am he that blotteth out thy transgressions for mine own sake, and will not remember thy sins" (Isaiah 43:25).

The Bible says in another place, "And their sins and iniquities will I remember no more" (Hebrews 10:17).

And in Hebrews 8:12 God says, "For I will be merciful to their unrighteousness, and their sins and their iniquities will I remember no more."

You are the righteousness of God in Christ. If God has no remembrance of your sins, why do you keep bringing it up?

The righteousness of God is through faith in Jesus Christ. As a matter of fact, if you up to this point of your life have not confessed Jesus as Lord and have not called on His name, can I say to you, Jesus is knocking at the door of your heart. My prayer for you is that you answer the door. If you answer the door and let Him in, Jesus will change your life for the better.

Don't try to clean up your house, which is your life, before you answer the door! I remember growing up as a little kid, and if someone was knocking at our door, I better not open that door unless my house was clean and in order, particularly the living room where we entertained company. But this is JESUS! Answer the door and let Him in because He (Jesus) has the power and ability to save you.

No man has the power or "G" type blood to save himself. Remember it's on you to let Him in. Jesus is not going to force His way into your house (life) because that would be breaking the law commonly called "B and E," which is the crime of breaking and entering. Jesus is knocking at the door of your heart. If you let Him in, Jesus said He and the Father will come and make their abode with you. (John 14:23)"

What every believer, child of God, should know and understand about the new creation in Christ is that the new creation is absolutely a life changing miracle. As a new creature you are a new spiritual species. You are a new person who has never existed before, though physically but not spiritually. Your physical body is not you; your body is the house that the real you (your spirit) lives in. You were created or should I say recreated in the image of God.

Wow, can you believe it? You are a new creation miracle!

ABOUT THE AUTHOR

Dr. Jerry Wilder, Sr. is the Founder and Senior Pastor of Grace and Restoration Fellowship Church located at 385 Broadway, Paterson, NJ. Dr. Wilder, Sr. refers to Paterson, NJ as the City of Righteousness.

Grace and Restoration Fellowship Church, is a place where everybody is somebody! A church where the unadulterated Word of God is taught; souls are saved, lives are changed, minds are renewed, people are empowered and transformed by the word of God and the power of the Holy Spirit. Dr. Jerry Wilder's assignment is to teach and preach the gospel of Christ with an emphasis on the message of faith because, "without faith it is impossible to please God" **(Hebrews 11:6)**.

Dr. Jerry Wilder, Sr., is married to Dr. Verdele Wilder. He is the father of six; three daughters and three sons. He received Jesus Christ as his personal Lord and Savior in August, 1983. His family motto is from the book of Joshua 24:15, which states; "As for me and my house, we will serve the Lord." Dr. Jerry Wilder's life verse is Hebrews 11:1: Now

Faith is the assurance (the confirmation, the title deed) of the things we hope for, being the proof of things we do not see and the conviction of their reality-faith perceiving as real fact what is not revealed to the senses (Amplified Bible). Dr. Jerry Wilder was raised in Paterson, N.J. (The city he calls "The City of Righteousness").

Dr. Jerry Wilder is a graduate of FFWOC (Faith Fellowship World Outreach Center) Bible school of ministry. He later attended the Alpha Bible Institute, where he obtained a bachelor's Degree in Religious Education, and a Master's Degree in Theology. Also, Dr. Wilder received a Doctorate Degree of Religious Education in June of 2008. The emphasis, focus and thrust of Dr. Jerry Wilder's ministry is to reach the destitute, the wounded, the broken-hearted, the discouraged, the bound, the uncommitted, the backslider, and the un-churched through the unadulterated, preaching and teaching of the gospel of the Lord Jesus Christ.

ORDER INFORMATION

You can order additional copies of The New Creation In Christ by emailing the author directly using the email address below.

Jerry Wilder, Sr.

Jerry.Wilder213@yahoo.com

Books are available at Amazon.com, BN.com Kindle and Your Local Bookstores (By Request)

Please leave a review for this book on Amazon and let other readers know how much you enjoyed reading it.

Thank you!

www.ingramcontent.com/pod-product-compliance
Lightning Source LLC
Chambersburg PA
CBHW070029110426
42741CB00035B/2698